NATIONAL GEOGRAPHIC

# Ladders

## WELCOME TO
## KENYA
### AROUND THE WORLD

# Welcome to KENYA!

by Stephanie Herbek

Kenya is a country in Africa. Most days there are hot, dry, and sunny. Cheetahs, elephants, giraffes, and many other animals live in Africa. They live on **savannas**, or lands covered with grasses and other plants. They find shade under trees. The leaves hide them from the hot sun.

These cheetahs live in the grassy savannas of Kenya. Cheetahs can run 70–75 miles an hour. Female cheetahs often have three babies at a time.

Animals aren't the only living things in Kenya. More than 40 million people live there, too. Most of them live in **villages**. A village is a community that is smaller than a city. A village is usually located in the country. Many people who live in villages work on farms. They plant crops in their fields.

Other Kenyans live in the city. They take a bus or drive cars to get to their jobs. They work in offices, factories, and schools. Let's find out more about the people and communities of Kenya.

# Straw Huts and Skyscrapers

The Kenyans in some villages live with their **tribes**. A tribe is a group of people with the same language and beliefs. Most villagers live in small huts made of sticks and mud. A fire pit in the middle of each hut is used to cook food. It is also used to heat water for washing. Villagers get water from deep underground wells.

Kenyan villagers keep very busy working on their farms. They grow much of the food they eat. One food they grow is cassava. Cassava is a vegetable that is a little like a potato. Villagers also care for their cows and goats. These animals give villagers milk to sell in markets and to drink.

Kenyan huts are designed well. Their straw roofs shelter people from the hot sun. Huts also keep villagers dry when it rains.

> People sell their crops and farm animals at markets. This colorful market is in the center of a Kenyan village.

Some Kenyans live in cities such as Nairobi (nih-ROH-bee). Nairobi is the capital of Kenya. It is the largest city in the country. More than three million people live there. This city has libraries, skyscrapers, and restaurants. Most people in Nairobi live in apartment buildings or houses made of metal. Some drive minivans. Others ride motorcycles or bikes.

> Some parts of Nairobi, Kenya, are green and full of trees. Other parts of the city are full of tall buildings and cars.

5

# Time for School, Time for Fun

Most children who live in Kenyan villages walk to school every morning. The day starts with a song. Then students learn Swahili (swuh-HEE-lee). This is the language that people speak in Kenya and in many other African countries. The students study outside at tables under trees. Sometimes they can hear birds chirping during their lessons. It must be fun to share a classroom with animals!

Not all children go to school in their village. Some of them go to schools far away from home. Other children help with farmwork instead of going to school.

Schools in the cities of Kenya are like many city schools in the United States. Some students wear uniforms to school. Others wear regular clothes. The children work at tables in large classrooms. At some city schools, students use computers. Just like you, students may walk or take a bus to and from school.

The weather in Kenya is sunny and warm. It is perfect for playing outside. What sports do Kenyan children play? They love to play soccer, basketball, and volleyball.

**tafadhali** (TAH-fah-DAH-lee) means "please"

**asante** (ah-SAHN-tay) means "thank you"

**Habari?** (hah-BAR-ee) means "How are you?"

**kwaheri** (kwah-HAIR-ee) means "good-bye"

Some classes in Kenya are held outdoors. Imagine seeing an elephant walk by while you are at school!

**Check In** How is school in Kenya different from what school is like where you live? How is it similar?

# Elephant and Hare

a Traditional Kenyan Folk Tale

*retold by Jenny Loomis*          *illustrated by Gerald Guerlais*

*A folk tale is a story that teaches **values**. Values are beliefs about what is important and how people should act. This folk tale is from Kenya. The elephant stands for strength. A **hare** is an animal like a rabbit. The Hare in the story stands for **cleverness**. If you have cleverness, you are smart. Some folk tales tell why animals look the way they do. This folk tale tells why hares have short tails.*

As day was turning to night, Hare stood at the edge of a river. She was looking down at the water. She needed to get home before Fox came out to hunt. Hare could shorten her trip home by crossing the river. But she wasn't strong enough to swim through the deep water.

Just then, Elephant came running across the field. He ran up to Hare and laughed. "I see you can't cross the river. That's too bad. Swimming is so easy for me!"

"Elephant, please wait," said Hare. "Could I ride on your back as you swim across the river? I'm afraid Fox will find me before I can get home. I need to give my children this big pot of honey." Hare showed Elephant the pot of honey in her basket.

Elephant smiled when he saw the honey. It was his favorite sweet treat. He could eat honey every day.

"I will carry you across the river if you give me your honey," Elephant said.

"But this honey is for my children," said Hare sadly.

"Fine. Then I am leaving. Say 'hello' to Fox for me," said Elephant meanly.

Hare knew she had to get home before dark. She quickly came up with a clever plan. "Okay, you can have the honey," said Hare.

"Great! Hop on so we can get going!" Elephant ordered.

Elephant carried Hare across the river. When they reached the other side, he lifted his trunk up over his head to get the honey pot. Instead, Hare put an empty cup into Elephant's trunk. Then she jumped off his back and ran toward her home. Elephant was busy looking at his powerful trunk. He didn't notice that Hare had fooled him.

When he saw he had been tricked, Elephant was angry. He threw the empty cup on the ground and ran after Hare. His strong legs took him closer and closer. Hare jumped into a hole. Elephant reached out and grabbed her long tail. Hare's long, fluffy tail snapped off. She was left with just a puff.

Elephant threw the tail down. He stuck his trunk into the hole to try to reach Hare. His trunk became caught in a tree root. Hare escaped while Elephant was busy trying to pull his trunk out. She ran to a large group of hares standing nearby.

Hare knew that she couldn't hide from Elephant for very long. She needed to look like the other hares, but they all had long tails. Then Hare had a clever idea. She hid her basket in some bushes and joined the group of hares. She yelled, "Quickly! Take off your long tails! Elephant is coming and he's very angry. He's looking for hares with long tails!"

The scared hares had just pulled off their long tails when Elephant arrived. He was very angry. He didn't like being tricked by a little hare. He wanted that honey now more than ever. He screamed, "I'm looking for the hare with the short tail!"

The group of hares slowly turned around. They showed Elephant their short tails.

"That hare has tricked me again!" grumbled Elephant. He was tired of clever hares. Elephant stomped away.

Hare picked up her basket and ran home as fast as she could. When she got there, she fed her hungry children the honey. Then she showed them her new, short tail. The children liked her short tail. They all shortened their own tails to match hers.

Hare also told her children about the elephant. "Children, you may not be as big and strong as other animals. But you are all very smart. When you get into trouble, think of a way out of it. Just being big or strong won't solve all your problems."

The children were glad they had such a smart mother. They each gave her a big hug. Then they ate the rest of the yummy honey.

**Check In**   How does Hare trick Elephant?

15

If you visit Kenya's savanna, you may see a man in bright red clothing walking through the grass. He's most likely a Maasai (muh-SY) man, walking with his cattle, or cows. The Maasai people live in Kenya. They are **nomads**, which means they move from place to place. They move to find fresh grass for their cows to eat.

Maasai men have to walk many miles each day. They must move their cattle to grassy areas.

# The Mighty M

The Maasai treat their cattle very well. Maasai men are usually in charge of the cattle. They often give their cows names. Sometimes they even sing to them! The Maasai think of their cows as family members. The cows give the Maasai what they need to live good lives. The Maasai get milk, meat, and leather from the cows. They are very useful animals.

*by Sean O'Shea*

# Milk, Meat, and Medicine

The Maasai don't eat their cows' meat very often. They only eat the meat at special times. The cows' milk is more important to the Maasai. Milk makes up most of their diet. Milk is a common meal for the Maasai. They also use milk to make other foods.

In the morning, some Maasai drink milk or spiced milky tea called *chai* (CHY). Many Maasai eat a meal made from corn flour, milk, water, and sugar. This meal is called *ugi*. The Maasai also eat yogurt made from their cows' milk.

Sometimes the Maasai nibble on tree bark. That might seem strange to you. But if you've eaten anything with cinnamon in it, you've eaten tree bark, too. You might add cinnamon to oatmeal. The Maasai also like to add flavor to food. They use tree bark to flavor soup. They also use bark as medicine for an upset stomach.

Owning cattle is a lot of work. Maasai men spend their days herding the animals. Maasai women milk the cattle twice a day.

## How to Make Kenyan Chai Tea

Chai tea is a very popular drink in Kenya. It is tea mixed with milk, sugar, and spices. Many children drink chai in the morning before going to school.

1. Pour 2 cups of water and 2 cups of milk into a saucepan.

2. Add 1½ teaspoons of black tea leaves (or more, if you like strong tea) to the water and milk in the saucepan.

3. Add some spices such as cinnamon, cardamom, and ginger to the saucepan.

4. With an adult's help, bring the mixture to a boil.

5. Turn the heat down and mix the tea with a spoon until it tastes strong enough.

6. Add a little sugar to sweeten the tea, and stir.

7. Remove the tea leaves from the saucepan.

8. Pour the spiced tea into a mug and enjoy!

# The Power of Red

The Maasai wear clothing that keeps them cool in Kenya's warm weather. Some of their clothing and shoes are made from animal skins. They also wear cotton because it keeps them cool. The Maasai's villages are far away from markets. They sometimes make clothes from things they find near their homes. Some Maasai even use old tires to make sandals. The Maasai like to wear bright colors. Red is an important color to them. It **symbolizes**, or stands for, power.

The Maasai make colorful jewelry. They use glass and clay beads as **ornaments**, or things that add beauty. They also string together metal, seeds, ivory, bone, horns, shells, leather, and feathers. The Maasai turn these things into earrings, necklaces, and bracelets. Sometimes young men and women wear jewelry to attract each other.

# Jumping for Joy

Jumping is part of a Maasai dance called *adumu*. In this dance, **warriors** take turns jumping. A Maasai warrior is a young man who learns how to hunt. He also learns how to keep his family safe. Each warrior sings as he jumps higher and higher. The man who jumps the highest wins the contest. The Maasai believe that the winner is the strongest warrior.

Maasai males become warriors when they are in their teens. They are warriors for about ten years. Then they are ready to become adults. They dance to celebrate the beginning of adulthood. Once they are adults, the men can get married. They can also have a family and raise cows.

Two Maasai warriors show their strength by jumping high into the air.

**Check In** Why are cattle important to the Maasai?

## Discuss

1.  Tell about some of the ways you think the three selections in this book are linked.

2.  How is living in a village in Kenya different from living in a city?

3.  What are some important things you have learned about the Maasai way of life?

4.  In the folk tale, Hare is clever and Elephant is strong. Do you think cleverness or strength is more important? Why?

5.  What do you still wonder about Kenya and the people who live there?